DARINGLY DISABLED

The adventures of Sheila-the-wreck

Sheila Taylor

Published in 2016 by
Clive Scoular
Killyleagh
County Down

ISBN 978-0-9574626-6-3

for the unsung heroes of
the emergency services and Samaritans
of Northern Ireland

who dedicate their lives to saving strangers

Contents

Introduction

Hello, I hope you will enjoy reading my book. It is about me, Sheila – the wreck!

I was badly disabled following a road traffic accident in 1996. My car was a wreck, and I am a wreck!

I hope you will find this book both light hearted and helpful. My aim is to encourage people like myself who are less-able for any reason, to realise that there are so many opportunities available for us to enjoy life, and to make the best of what we are able to do.

When I handed over my script to Clive Scoular and Thomas Johnston, I could not believe my luck. I didn't know how it would be received but I needn't have worried for they have been not only hard working and professional, but have been kind, positive and, yes, patient with me. I owe them a debt of gratitude as well as my sincere thanks and appreciation.

All proceeds from the sale of this book will go to Bangor and North Down Samaritans. They have always been there for me, and they will be for you too.

Happy reading.

Sheila Taylor

Holywood, February 2016

Foreword

Samaritans was founded in November 1953 by Dr Chad Varah CH, CBE. The idea for the service was sown after he had conducted the funeral of a 14-year-old girl who had taken her own life after she had started menstruating and thought she was gravely ill. Chad vowed at her graveside to devote himself to helping other people to overcome the sort of isolation and ignorance that had caused the girl to die in this way. He would do it through a combination of education and the provision of access to emotional support in times of need.

When he was offered charge of the parish of St Stephen Walbrook in London in the summer of 1953, Chad knew that the time was right for him to launch what he called '999 for the suicidal'. At that time suicide was illegal and many people who were in difficult situations and who felt suicidal were unable to talk to anyone about it without worrying about the possible consequences. A confidential emergency service for people 'in distress' was what Chad Varah felt was needed to address the problems he saw around him. The first call to the service was made on 2 November 1953 and this date became recognised as Samaritans' official birthday.

As of 2016 Samaritans has over 200 branches in the UK and Ireland. The aim of the charity is to provide emotional support for people who are struggling to cope, and who are experiencing suicidal thoughts. Samaritans is entirely volunteer-led and completely dependent on the good hearts, motivation, commitment and hard work of its 22,000 volunteers.

Sheila 793 (all volunteers are given a number) is one such remarkable volunteer. She has been with the Bangor and North Down branch of Samaritans since 1998. When Sheila asked me to write the foreword for her book, I was a little taken aback. Despite the fact that Sheila's presence in the branch is often indicated by her trademark mobility scooter which she leaves at the front door, there is nothing, to my mind, about Sheila that suggests any lack of ability in any sense – quite the contrary.

Whilst I have known Sheila for as long as I have been in the branch, I did not get to know her properly until I became the branch Director. It was then that I discovered how much she knows about all the machinations of running the Bangor and North Down branch and just how much she keeps an eye on things. I have had many a helpful hint from her as to things that needed to be attended to.

Samaritans is dependent on there being sufficient volunteers on duty so as to be there for the callers who so badly need us. A key role in our branch is that of our rota-minder and Sheila has responsibility for co-ordinating the small team of volunteers who take turns every week to ensure that all our shifts are covered. The rota-minders variously cajole, persuade or charm volunteers into putting themselves on for an extra shift when needed. The branch rota is online but Sheila's lack of a computer or access to the Internet at home is no barrier to her managing the rota. If she can't get into the branch, she will go to her local library or commandeer the facilities of anyone with whom she is staying, as she did at Christmas past when on holiday visiting family. Sheila tells us in her book about picking up computer skills when she started going to the Bayview Centre following her dreadful accident. This is just one example of how Sheila's forward-looking positivity has benefitted others in need.

Sheila's book is a joy to read. It is inspirational, uplifting, frank and funny. She starts her story after her life-changing car accident in 1996 when she sustained horrendous injuries. I didn't know Sheila before her accident but I rather suspect that when Sheila's physical disabilities diminished, her intellectual acuity, spirit and emotional strength increased commensurately. At one point after her accident, Sheila tells us 'well, I said to myself – I can see, I can hear and I can talk'. And it is with those faculties that Sheila has continued her life in a way that many a more able bodied person could only dream of.

Sheila's exploits, travels and experiences read like a 20 year old's bucket list of things to do before they die. Sheila has opted to ride an elephant, when her companions preferred to shop; to swim with dolphins; to go snorkelling and off-road driving in Havana; to water ski at Craigavon and to join the crew of the *Lord Nelson* when she achieved her three objectives – to navigate, to climb up to the crow's nest and to become the Captain's mate.

The kindness of others characterises many of Sheila's experiences. She has had no shortage of companions and helpers, and at times has put herself into the care of complete strangers with seemingly no concern about anything going amiss. Her belief in the inherent goodness of people is evident throughout her story and it seems that she has been rewarded in the people she has come across in her travels who have helped her to participate in the many activities that she was so clearly determined to enjoy.

When Sheila was a child she imagined that she was a seagull, because no one eats seagulls and seagulls never falter nor stall. I believe that was rather prophetic because, despite the knocks that Sheila has sustained (and not all of them are in her book), it doesn't seem that she ever faltered or stalled – and she certainly has never been eaten!

I am very grateful to Sheila for donating the proceeds from her book to the Bangor and North Down branch of Samaritans. Someone contacts Samaritans every six seconds. People don't have to be suicidal to call Samaritans. Whatever a person is going through, they can contact Samaritans for free any time of the day. I am sure that Sheila's story will give hope and inspiration to many who may themselves have suffered a similar life-changing event and who wonder how they are going to go forward.

Deirdre Walsh

Director – Bangor and North Down Samaritans

February 2016

A message from Anne Hailes MBE

In July 2002 I interviewed Sheila Taylor for the *Irish News*. Sitting in her cosy flat in Holywood, county Down, the story she told me was one of extreme courage and determination because, only six years previously, on the narrow road between Comber and Moneyreagh, she was involved in a horrific crash that put her in hospital for ten months. Many thought it was the end for Sheila, an active, engaging woman whose career in nursing had taken her from Belfast to becoming head nurse in a Saudi Arabian hospital and then working for a member of the Saudi royal family, before coming home to Northern Ireland with her husband to lay down roots. The year of the crash had started well and life was good with five grandchildren, a nursing home job she loved and a happy family life.

It all changed that morning in 1996 on that twisty and dangerous county Down road when she had to be cut out of her car which ended up underneath a lorry. She was never expected to walk again after the trauma but, thanks to the staff and consultants at the Royal Victoria Hospital, her body was literally put together again and her sight restored. Sheila then took over, called their bluff, discharged herself and got on with life.

You will be impressed with her zest for life, her physical adventures and, above all, her sense of survival, good humour and fun.

With her typical generosity all proceeds from this book will go to help the work of Bangor and North Down Samaritans.

Sheila, you told me you called yourself Sheila the Wreck! More like a wrecking ball that demolished every obstacle in its path to allow new horizons to open up.

Anne Hailes MBE

Belfast

February 2016

One
The day Sheila's life changed

It all happened one Friday in February 1996 when I was working for Crestacare. I was travelling from Donacloney clinic to Croagh Patrick clinic in Donaghadee along a twisty country road from Carryduff towards Comber. Two lorries were coming towards me. There was a high grass bank on my side of the road and open fields on the other. I tried to keep over to my side of this narrow road but I got stuck in a broken tarmacadam rut that had been caused by the snow, frost and ice over the winter months.

As I was trying to correct my position, I over-corrected, and went under the first lorry. The driver was not hurt, but as far as I was concerned I do thank the Lord I didn't remember anything after that. I later discovered that my car engine had been pushed forward and had crushed both my feet.

It took the firemen three hours to remove my car roof after which they decided, because I was still wedged in, to cut the car in half and remove me backwards. Only then could they get me into the ambulance.

I was taken to the Ulster Hospital, Dundonald. In order to stem the internal bleeding I was taken to theatre to have my spleen removed. As I was still bleeding, it was decided that I should be transferred to the Royal Victoria Hospital in Belfast. I was informed where they were taking me but needless to say I cannot confirm this owing to my critical condition. They waited until the rush hour was over and then closed off the roads to ensure my speedy transfer to the Royal Victoria. There were police in front and behind the ambulance to make the journey as smooth as possible. It sounded as if I was treated like royalty. That evening I was taken to theatre to repair my liver which was causing my continued internal bleeding.

I was in intensive care for many weeks. I understand I had sixteen operations in twenty-three days. I don't recall any of this; I know I did not sign any forms; I know I did not give my permission. As far as I understand it they just helped themselves! I was attached to nine machines, which meant I needed two nurses with me twenty-four hours a day.

I was still unconscious when they needed my bed, and the intensive care staff felt they could do no more for me. So I was transferred to the orthopaedic ward, where the staff were informed that I was a patient with so many fractures that they did not expect me to survive.

When I eventually regained consciousness, there was a physiotherapist working on my feet. I asked her what I was doing here, and she told me I had been involved in a serious road accident. I then noticed that I had eight fixators in both legs; a large dressing on my left knee; six fixators in my right arm, and my left arm was in plaster of Paris. I also had had a tracheotomy; a tube for feeding me through my nose, and a catheter and urine bag were in place. Well, I thought – I can see, I can hear, and I can talk. I remember regaining consciousness on Good Friday, when a huge bouquet of flowers arrived for me from the Ulster Bank on the Ormeau Road. It was many months before I could write. I had to go down to the Occupational Therapy Unit to learn to use my disabled left hand. The first letter I wrote was to the bank manager, to thank him for the beautiful flowers, which were totally unexpected and were enough to make anyone regain consciousness by receiving such an unexpected gift, and especially from the bank – many thanks to the bank manager.

After a few days I asked to see the dietician and occupational therapist. No one asked why, but they came in the afternoon. I spoke to the dietician about the yoghurt. She assured me she could only give me what had been ordered for me, but they had soon learnt that if they tried to give me something I didn't like, I looked straight at the nurse and spat it in her face! I told the dietician that I did like the yoghurt, but there were no teaspoons on the ward, and the staff had been trying to feed me a Petits Filous, which was in a small pot, with a big spoon. After that they made sure to get teaspoons with 'Sheila' taped to them. I said to the O.T. that I couldn't be the only disabled patient in the hospital who wanted to help herself. My left thumb and first finger only opened a small amount, and I found that the ward glasses were far too heavy for me. I knew I only wanted a little water in the glass to get a sip of water when I wanted it, and not to have to ask for help and get far too much shoved down me in one go. So the next day a light plastic tommee tippee cup was brought to me, which enabled me to learn to help myself.

The physiotherapists worked very hard on me, three times a day, and even at the weekends when they really were only available for emergencies and the very sick.

Once the fixators were unscrewed and removed from my legs and arm, I was taken down to the hydrotherapy pool. The first time there were two physios to ensure all went well. I was left on a canvas seat to exercise my legs and after that I was able to hold on to the side rail and kick my legs forwards and backwards. Before long I was able to stand and kick my feet out of the water in front of me. The physios could not believe it. Since I was so contented in the water I was invariably the first patient down in the morning and there I stayed until lunchtime.

It was about this time, on a ward round, that the consultant told me I had 56 fractures, and with two disabled feet and a disabled right arm, I must be prepared to be wheelchair bound. I remember asking the consultant who was asked to count all my fractures, and he replied 'Sheila, I took all your x-rays home and counted all your fractures myself'.

Shortly after this, the physiotherapists came into my room with a new walking aid, and asked if I was happy for them to see if it would work for me. This frame was on wheels and had arm supports that enabled me to hold the grips to take as much weight off my feet as my arms would allow. The physio had some control behind me, in case I went too fast or needed her support. We practised this for a few days, and then it was a Tuesday, the boss's ward round. I said to the physios that I would wait until he was in the six-bedded bay next door, and then I would go in. They said 'Sheila, you can't do that!' 'Just watch me!' I replied. So when the doctors, the sister with her trolley, and the occupational therapist arrived, I waddled in, wearing just my shorts and a t-shirt, with my new machine. The 'boss' (my pet name for my consultant) just stood open mouthed. 'Good morning to you, Sir, I have come to join your ward round, to ensure that all is going well, before you come next door to me'. The boss sat down, and everyone just roared with laughter. I could not stand any longer, so I waddled off. When the boss came in to me, he said he never expected to see me on my feet, let alone wanting to join in his ward round.

Whenever the ward sister came in contact with me, it was just like waving a red rag to a bull. As soon as a single room became available, I was moved into it, out of the way. Eventually my own wheelchair arrived. In the mornings I would get myself ready for swimming and get my wheelchair out into the corridor. Sister would say 'What are you doing out here?' I said 'Did you not know this is a bus stop. I am waiting for a bus to be taken swimming'. She didn't dare tell me to go back to my room for I was not in the way. If she had I would have got myself out of the ward. My consultant was a quiet man, and with his patient being a bit boisterous, we got on very well. When coming into my single room he would invariably say 'Well what are you going to tell me this week?' I told him I had got a scooter – this was in the late 1990s when mobility scooters were only just coming to the fore. The consultant asked 'How fast does it go?' I said 'four to six miles an hour, Sir.' 'And how far does it go?' I replied that I had just been looking at my map, and it will go from my house in Donaghadee to yours in Helen's Bay, no problem!' Sister piped up and said 'How do you think you will be able to get home from doctor's house?' 'Get home' said I, 'once I am at the boss's house, to pot with my ruddy scooter!' You can imagine how the other doctors, physios and O.T.s laughed. But the sister never learnt. For some reason or other she objected to me being the centre of attention for three to four minutes a week. The next week I informed the boss that I had decided I didn't need a bath. I needed to be groomed because my legs were so hairy. He said that was because I had been so ill for so long and it was nature's way of trying to keep me warm. But he still was not able to provide a currycomb or a dandy brush to provide this patient with her needs.

One day there was a knock on my door, and in came one of the administrators in a dark suit, and said that UTV would like to interview me and would I be prepared to be interviewed'. I said 'I was happy to talk to anyone'. They opened the door and there was Jane Loughrey, lights and cameras and all. I was just as I was, dressed only in shorts and a t-shirt, without socks and slippers because of my wounds. The interview was on road safety (ha, ha) and seat belts. I was then asked 'Why did I think I had been rehabilitated as well as I had?' I replied it was probably 50% due to the medical staff, and 50% to me. But the hospital staff said that that was rubbish, as 98% was due to me. Who was I to argue? I then had to show them how to walk with no heels and no ankles and, with my one crutch, I waddled off down the corridor. It was on the television the next night. I received fan mail addressed to the 'Miracle Walker', and it found me.

I was never officially discharged from hospital. During one ward round I told the boss that I was going home at the weekend, and he said 'Sheila, if you want to go home for the weekend, no trouble'. I said 'No, I have been in hospital long enough and it's time for me to go home'. He replied that when he visited me each week, and was told by the physios I was getting stronger, he wanted me to stay. But I did leave the hospital and it was arranged that I would come to the Royal twice a week for hydrotherapy, and to the Ards Hospital for physiotherapy three times a week.

I just have to be so thankful to the staff at the Royal Victoria Hospital. Everyone was so kind and patient with me. I am sure that if I had been treated in any other hospital, it would be doubtful if it would have had all the facilities available for me. The consultant continued to see me at outpatients for twelve years. He was interested in the activities I was able to partake in with my two disabled feet and my one fused arm that did not feed me, or wash me, or brush my hair, although it did help me to pull up my pants!

Two
Bayview Resource Centre

In 1999 I was offered a place at Bayview. It was very difficult walking into a strange place, where you knew no one and had to go into a dining room for coffee or tea. And trying to find a seat was almost impossible – 'Friends sit here', 'this table is full'. Eventually I found a table with another new start, and so Joe and I sat down together, and we are still friends.

The aim of the resource centre is to try to encourage people to make the best use of what they can do in the hope that they can return to a full life. Some users do try to learn new skills, whilst some just sit around. You get out of Bayview what you put into it.

I had never touched a computer until Bayview got two of them. There were eight in the computer group, and we were asked to write down our names and addresses. But you could be sure that before you had completed your task, you would be pushed off the computer because someone else wanted a go.

Our new manager introduced swimming sessions. Eight of us were taken to the Bangor Leisure Centre and, because of my time at the Royal Victoria Hospital, I found I could keep myself afloat trying to do the breaststroke, but I got nowhere. My feet, which were fixed at 90°, meant that they were holding me back. No one can tell you how to swim when they don't have your disabilities. I tried to swim on my back, and developed the Bayview bum stroke, when I took my arms above my head, with my feet doing a frog like movement, and this did enable me to move, albeit slowly.

To get into the pool they had a hoist, which I always used. As they were putting me in, the water would always seem cold. As soon as my feet hit the water, I would splash and shout and say that the water was cold, have you forgotten to put the heating on? The school children in their own pool nearby would stop their lesson and watch me. One of the male swimming attendants would leave me half in the water, on the hoist. As I continued to shout and splash, he just left me. I told him he was here to be nice to me, and not give me a hard time. He assured me that there was nothing in his contract that said he had to be nice to Sheila! So I don't think I won that one.

Bayview had a creative writing class. I joined this group, and at the first session we were given taffeta. We could screw

With my friends, Cathy the carer and Jeanette the chef, in the kitchen at Bayview

it up or do whatever we wanted with it and then write about the things that went through our minds. Another time we were asked to write about our trip to Bayview that morning. I said I had come over Craigantlet and talked about the trees, the forest, the horses, and the fishermen at the lake. The next week you were asked to write about all the bad things on that trip. Another very revealing session was asking people to draw or write to say how they saw themselves. I wanted to be an orange tree because it was in fruit and blooming at the same time. Another chap, who had suffered a stroke, drew a tree broken in half by a storm. That made me think. Some of Bayview's writings are on the walls in the Ulster Hospital.

The original Bayview was a building overlooking the beach, which had been built as a residential home. The rooms were inclined to be small. As time went by the roof started to cause problems, and it was apparent that Bayview was going to have to find alternative accommodation. I was asked to be on the committee to discuss the centre's future, and we talked and discussed for two or more years. Eventually Clifton School for children with learning disabilities moved to a new location with plenty of grounds near Clandeboye. This enabled Bayview to knock down Clifton School's old property on the Ballyholme Road plus the building next door, Kyle House, which belonged to the Health Authority who used it as offices. Eventually we formed an interview panel consisting of the architect, the Health Estates builder, an electrician, and, on behalf of the users, a representative each for the elderly, those with learning disabilities, a mental health worker, and myself representing the disabled.

I had never been in this situation before being part of a team deciding who should be given the task of building the new Bayview. The eight Health Authority team members sat on one side, and then we started to interview some big international firms. They also had eight on their team. They showed us videos, and talked about their plans. After an hour or so they left and

With Diane and John, checking the activiy schedule.

then we had to fill in the scores we felt each firm had warranted on the various topics.

As a team we then moved next door where the next new company was waiting for us. We worked like this for two days starting at 8.30am. We eventually gave the job to a local firm. So that really was an eye opener to me, to see how these big firms worked and how they were financed with their talk of budgets of millions of pounds. My one contribution to the new Bayview plan was to recommend that they did not forget to have the toilet close to the entrance because members attending the centre would have been on the bus for quite a while and most would have been taking water pills. Therefore a toilet near to the entrance was essential. The architect said 'Thank you Sheila, I had never realised the need for that before'. He will when he gets older!

I am now a volunteer at Bayview, and am also on the Users Forum which meets every six weeks.

The valuable skills I learned during my time at Bayview were computer skills, swimming and creative writing. As I said at the beginning, you get out of Bayview what you put into it.

Three

Ten wheelchair users in Thailand

I decided that I could not continue to live my life in sheltered accommodation without making some effort to get out and meet other people. So in 2000 I came across a company on the internet that took small groups of disabled people on exotic holidays. So I signed up for Thailand.

The flight lasted 13 hours, and I coped with that. There were ten of us in the group and we were in the centre section of the plane, behind the galley, with business class in front. So this meant that no one was far from the toilet. The airline staff had a narrow canvas seat that they used to get those of us unable to walk, over to the toilet. They opened the door wide, locked it up against the business class wall, and then they had a wide curtain that enabled help to be given as and when needed. I often wondered how they coped with these things on aeroplanes.

A happy group, including my friend, Jim

Once we arrived in Bangkok we had a luxurious coach with a side lift for wheelchairs. We only had two carers with us, so two local boys were hired and they stayed with us all the time. We had an interpreter and driver. One of our group members was Jim who had cerebral palsy and he had his own carer, Andy. Jim could not eat or drink without help. One night we were in a bar in the Amari Hotel and I said I would get the drinks. I could not leave Jim out, so, after taking everyone else's order, I asked Jim what he would like. He said he wanted Bacardi and coke. I said 'Jim, do you really mean it, because I will get it for you?' So I fed Jim his Bacardi and coke through a straw. I said to him 'Take it easy, because I don't want to drown you'. He did cough and splutter, but we did laugh. We got most of it down him before his nurse, Andy, returned. That did put a big smile on Jim's face.

Bangkok is a very busy, hot and dusty city although the temples are magnificent. We visited the Royal Palace with the Emerald Buddha. This is the most revered temple in Thailand and was built in 1782. A lot of the temples are made of gold, and all the other walls and buildings are covered in mosaic.

One evening we went on a 'Wine and Dine' cruise down the river Chao Phraya. The river is huge. We had seven individual dishes for each course. By night Bangkok looks superb with all its temples lit up, making lovely reflections on the river. The first class hotels are also well illuminated, thus adding to the atmosphere.

One night we went to the night market. It was very crowded and on a cobbled hill. The night-time temperature was 90°F. I am not one for shopping unless I want something, so I said to Nuu, who was my Thai carer pushing me, 'let's get out of here'. So we went down the hill on to the main road. Its street surface was not much better and the pavements were very high and uneven. But Nuu and I just strolled along. I noticed there was a pedestrian area on my left, well lit up and with the trees decorated. Tables

A lovely evening meal

Drinks beside the swimming pool

and chairs were set out, with lots of music. So I said to Nuu that we should go along there. I noticed then that 'Live Sex' bars were inviting you in but I pretended I had not realised that we were in the 'red light' district. So we strolled along until we got to the end. When we turned round, a good-looking young man came up and stood by my chair. He introduced himself and asked if I had ever been in one of these bars. I assured him I had not. He said 'Come on, I will take you in'. I said 'No, I could not do that as I was with a group of disabled folk and we have to meet the bus'. 'What time do you have to meet the bus?' When I said 2am, he said that we had plenty of time. So he took us into this bar. No lights - only neon lights picking out the white shirts - and all men! Boys came and picked up my chair and put it right beside a kind of boxing ring in the middle. On the wall was a video of boys kissing. My new friend asked me what I wanted to drink. I felt safe with a bottle of beer.

My new friend sat beside me and asked me my name. He laughed when I said 'Sheila' because he came from Australia. I said 'OK, so you are well blessed with millions of Sheilas'. On to the stage came six boys, wearing sarongs. Thank goodness, because I was right beside the ring! They had candles and danced slowly and sensually, but no one could take exception to their performance. This meant that the wall video could now be turned off. I said to my friend, 'Just looking at these young boys, you have to admire them as they are all very attractive. I was thinking what turmoil these young lads had to endure before they decided this was what they wanted from life'. My friend agreed with me, because he himself had to make this decision. He had come over to Bangkok when he was 17 years old, because his parents could not accept his sexuality. I asked him how old he was now and he told me that he was 35 years old and worked in an office. He asked how old I was and he laughed and said I was older than his mother. I reminded him that he had found me, and that I was not looking for him! I then offered to buy us another beer and Nuu got them and brought them over.

When it was time to go, the boys came along and lifted me up. I was most surprised when my friend walked me all the way back to the road before giving me a hug and a kiss, and thanked me for my company. He must have enjoyed our time together otherwise he probably would have just left me at the front door.

When we got back to the bus, the others all asked where I had been, as they could not see me at the market. I said we just went and cased the area. But where did you go? I looked at Nuu, hoping he would keep quiet, but he couldn't do that. 'We went to a gay bar, and they liked me more than Sheila!' You can imagine the organisers were not too impressed with my evening's entertainment!

We then moved from Bangkok to Pattaya. It was two and a half hours by coach to the fabulous 5 star accommodation where we were staying. We were then taken on a visit to a school for the disabled which had been started by Father Ray Brennan, an American priest, in 1974 for the street children and orphans. Then it had 170 children. He later started a school for the deaf and another for the blind. The school for the disabled had 200 students aged 17 to 34 years. They are taught computer studies and electronics and they all learn English. They say 100% of their students find employment. One of the seventeen-year-old boys welcomed us in English, and said he had been at the school for six months. I spoke out and thanked him for welcoming us, and for being so brave as to do it in our language. Our Jim said 'Yes, he speaks better than me'. I could have cried.

We had one free day, so people could do what they wanted. Most wanted to shop, but I went to the hotel reception and told them I wanted to ride an elephant. They rang up and arranged for a jeep to come and pick me up. So I was taken to a farm in the jungle where the elephants were. As I was on my own, I had to climb up wooden steps on to a platform that enabled you to step off on to the elephant seat that can take two or three people. I sat in the middle and the driver sat on the elephant's neck. The elephants travel slowly and stop and eat whenever they want. We came to a river and in went the elephant and the water was up to his eyes. I suppose he breathed through his trunk. When we returned to the platform, it was too far away for me to get up and cross the gap without help. So I just shouted 'help, help', and eventually they came and got me off. It had been a wonderful experience, and I was so glad that I had the courage to go off on my own. I was able to show everyone the photograph taken of me swimming on an elephant.

Another scrumptious meal

A Bangkok soldier on guard

A golden temple in Bangkok

We were all together by the swimming pool, but sitting under the palm trees in the shade. I asked everyone if they would like an ice cream. Only Andy, Jim's nurse, said 'Yes'. So off I went and got two chocolate cornets. I waddled slowly back to our group and, with the daytime temperature of 90°F, the ice cream had already started to melt. All the guests were laughing and saying in different languages, 'You like chocolate!' By the time I reached Andy I was covered in ice cream down each arm, down my legs and across my tummy. After eating our ice creams, our faces were also smothered. We said 'What are we going to do? We can't go in the pool. We can't go into the hotel'. We then saw the shower. So before a large audience of guests and staff, Andy and I got into the shower together, gave a good show of bathing together, and helped each other as well as we could, if you know what I mean! We received a hearty ovation from all our observers. We both bowed, before returning to our group.

On the way home, I thought how lucky we had been to have got on so well. I began to think about those who weren't even able to enjoy a cup of tea or a lovely festive dinner at Christmas time. Everyone else just takes all this for granted. But for disabled folk we must be thankful that we can look after ourselves pretty well and can lead lives which are reasonably full and normal. We can dream and be loved for who we are.

Four

Samaritans

I contacted Samaritans in the spring of 1998 to enquire about becoming a volunteer. I was told that the spring training had just started and so I would need to wait until September, as there was paperwork to be completed, and I would also need to be interviewed. I do remember my interview, held in the downstairs back room, with me sitting with my crutch between my legs. It could never be said they did not know that I was disabled.

Our training took place in the YMCA along by Bangor Marina. Patrick was at the door, and enquired if I was attending Samaritans. When I said 'Yes', he looked at me, and I looked at him – because he had paperwork for me. I had my crutch in my good hand, as my other hand does not hold things. So Patrick did just the right thing – he pulled out my anorak and shoved the papers inside. There were eleven in our group of all

Sheila collecting on the streets of Bangor

ages. I could not help but notice that there were these young people, who had jobs, had families, were financially committed and yet were prepared to give four or five hours a week, and one night per month, to working with Samaritans. The training was on Monday evenings, and at the end, on one Saturday. We were taught about callers, what to expect, and how to encourage them to talk about their feelings, their fears and their concerns. We were at no time to talk about ourselves.

After we completed our training, we were invited to go into the centre and observe the workings of the office. If we felt confident enough after three observations we could start taking calls. You never started doing anything until you felt confident to do so.

There are many roles for Samaritans to make the centre work. We all take telephone calls and talk to anyone who comes to the centre wanting someone to talk to, and we offer them tea or coffee and biscuits. Our duty companion comes down after a while to ensure that the volunteer is comfortable and then I can ask for a cup of coffee. It is brought to me, as I am unable to carry my own tray because I need both hands to pull myself up the stairs. We need to go into the streets to collect money on flag days and it is when you are out in the street that you get your positive feedback from people saying 'If it was not for you ---'. We also have a specially trained Outreach team which visits schools and gives talks whenever invited to do so. Samaritans also have stands at musical fetes and country fairs. Samaritans walk around at these activities in case someone wants to talk. They also visit prisons on a regular basis. If you can teach, you can join the training team; if you can count, you can be involved in statistics or counting the cash raised in tins. The committee has to meet regularly and there is a team to organise the rotas. So there are many tasks volunteers can undertake if they are willing.

I found when I became ill that Samaritans had discovered that I had no family in Ireland. They knew one of my sons was in

Volunteers outside Samaritans Bangor office with the Mayor

Canada and the other in England, so they must have arranged a rota, to ensure that a Samaritan was at the Ulster Hospital every afternoon to be with me. They took my laundry, and must have decided who was to return it the next day. One Monday I went to theatre and was discharged home the following Monday. As I could not sit alone in my flat in Holywood, I got up and took the train with my scooter to the centre in Bangor. I entered the office and two girls were at the table and Alan was working on the computers. So when I walked in, Frances and Irene said 'Sheila, what the heck are you doing here? We didn't expect to see you for weeks'. They got me a cup of tea and asked me what way they had opened me up during my operation. I replied 'I have no idea because I could not see down there, because parts of my body were in the way!' So I stood up, pulled up my jumper, and lowered my trousers. Oh we did laugh! Two ladies and one man in the office; no modesty, and having to go to Samaritans just for them to see how I had been opened up!

We knew that Samaritans were going online to answer emails from all around the world. This was going to be a new role for them. Although I had learned some basic computer skills at Bayview Resource Centre, I did not feel competent enough to participate in this new computer scheme. So I decided to attend some further classes at Learndirect on Market Street in Bangor and I was their first disabled student. They were very good and patient with me and Lady Sylvia Herman, our local MP, came to see me. Some local newspaper and UTV reporters came along which gave Learndirect some welcome publicity. When the day arrived in October for us to send our first email, Mary was my companion that day. She said 'Sheila, do you think we can send an email?' I replied 'Mary, we can do anything!' In those days we would receive the email and print out two copies. We each sat at the desk and worked out our reply, and then together we decided what were the important points to respond to. Times are different now. One of us usually drafted the response, and then asked our companion if they were happy with the reply. We both needed to agree that the response was right for the caller, before it was sent. It seemed both wise and necessary to have two volunteers responding to emails.

Samaritans fill an important hole in my life. They give me a reason to leave my flat, as I am now part of a team and expected to be on duty regularly. They have always been there for me, but I hope this enables me to be there for people who are in distress and who need someone to talk to, and hopefully to reassure them that they are not alone. I always tell new volunteers this as we learn to work together.

A group of Samaritans volunteers and visiting choir at Sainsburys – we collected £700!

Five
The *Lord Nelson*

One day in Bayview, which overlooks Ballyholme beach, I looked out and saw yachts and other sailing ships passing by and making good use of the prevailing wind. I had always enjoyed boats, and particularly long boats, so I wondered how I could get on board a sailing ship. I went online and found the Jubilee Sailing Trust.

They own the *Lord Nelson* which is based at Southampton and it was the first sailing ship in the world designed to carry physically disabled people, as half of her crew. She was built in 1984 and her decks are all level and complete with lifts to enable the wheelchair crew to move around and participate in the running of the ship. The *Lord Nelson*'s owners are keen supporters of the annual Tall Ships race which visits different ports in all parts of the world. So I signed up in the spring of 2001.

The crew of the Lord Nelson

*The toilet and shower room on
board was very narrow!*

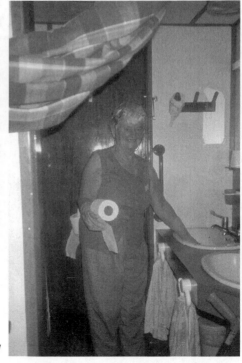

Me cleaning the toilet area!

The ship has ten permanent crew, plus twenty able-bodied and twenty disabled voluntary crew members. Each disabled member has an able-bodied buddy and they share cabins and the same watch. In fact they live together twenty-four hours a day. The *Lord Nelson* can cater for eight wheelchairs. There is an audio compass for the visually impaired and a braille one for the blind available on the bridge.

I was the only crew member without a buddy. Everyone else came in pairs and the disabled brought along family members, friends and carers, and there was one physiotherapist. So the Jubilee Sailing Trust kindly provided me with a buddy, Jean. She was of a similar age to me, and she knew we were both going to be working together, sharing the same two berth cabin together and being on watch together. She was there to help me in any way I needed and if we went ashore, she would help me with my wheelchair. She would also help me put on my wet gear once we were on deck.

We were divided into four watches, with ten crew members on each watch. The tasks were allocated to the more disabled first, then to those whose disability was less severe, and finally to the physically able-bodied. The watch leaders were also volunteers, as they had been regular sailors and trained so as to be able to encourage the rest of their team to complete any task allotted to them at any particular time. Our team leader was a

G.P., Dr Ian, and he was also the official doctor for this trip. He brought along his friend, Dr Alan, who was also a G.P. who was on his first trip. This proved to be a real sharing partnership.

When my application form arrived, one of the questions was 'Do you use your wheelchair always, some of the time or occasionally?' I replied by saying 'Occasionally, but always to the pub and back!' The next question was 'Can you climb a steep ladder with a hand rail on each side?' I thought who on earth has tried to climb a steep ladder, with or without handrails, when you are disabled? And so I replied 'I haven't a clue, but I will give it a go'. Then I was asked 'What do you hope to gain from this adventure?' I noted that they did not say 'holiday', because it certainly wasn't going to be that. I replied 'I hoped to navigate; I hoped to climb up to the crow's nest; and I hoped to become the Captain's mate. But not all in the first twenty-four hours'.

Accommodation on board was basic. There was very little storage space so you were told only to carry a sports bag and not a case. The fo'c'sle was where most of the crew slept. The bunks were three high, with baggage stored under the bottom bunk. The bunks were very close together and, when turning over at night, you were very likely to hit the bottom of the person above. There was no privacy and no doors, except on the toilets, as you can't have doors banging with the movement of the ship. Male and female crew members all mixed together. The eight wheelchair crew members were in the middle of the ship and their cabins were double ones, so there was more room. They were situated on the outer side of the boat with the toilets and washrooms in the middle. The toilets were very narrow so that there was never any danger of falling off in rough weather. This was also a shower with a half door, and you had to undress and put your clothes over the door, and then close the shower curtain. There was just room enough for you to stand and wash yourself. But don't think about drying because the floors were wet, the toilet was wet and the walls were wet. You just got your towel, looked around, and dashed to your bunk, and pulled the curtain.

On the first morning Bob, the first mate, introduced us to the crew. The captain, George Mills, had a meeting each morning with the permanent crew and watch leaders. The plans for the day were discussed, and this information passed on to the voluntary crew by their watch leaders. We were told to be sensible with regard to seasickness. There were stugeron tablets in the first aid box on each deck and we were advised to take them sooner rather than later. If you were being sick overboard, you made sure you chose the correct side. There were sickness bags available on each deck and if you were sick on the floor, you had to clean up after yourself for there was no one else to clean up after you. Safety harnesses were to be worn by all crew on deck thus enabling you to clip on to metal fittings during rough weather. They did work well, and gave you confidence when hoisting the sails in rough weather. Wet gear was not to be worn below deck, as it was noisy and would disturb the sleeping crew members. Alarm clocks were not permitted. Crew members were to be wakened by those on watch at night. All bunks were provided with PVC heel cloths, which protected the lower bunks, and stopped people falling out in rough weather.

The *Lord Nelson* was going nowhere until the crew had learned to handle the sails. On the first day after 'smokoo', which was our twice-daily coffee/tea break, there boomed over the intercom 'All able-bodied up the mast now'. Seventy per cent of the crew had been up the mast before, so they just ran up quite happily. All the crew, lads and lasses of all ages, worked together, and climbed aloft together, without any safety harnesses for they had to be free to move and clamber as instructed.

I noticed that there were two ladders going up to the crow's nest, with rigging on both sides, so I said to the bosun 'Cyril, can I have a go?' I don't know what made me want to do it, but the first task was to get me onto the ledge, which was waist high, to enable me to get onto the first step of the rigging. Cyril said 'Sheila, if you want a go, that's fine'. They found some boxes, and with some willing help from the crew, I was on the bottom rung. But with my disabled feet and disabled hand it was hard to cope with the large gap between each step. We had no safety harness and there was nothing between the sea and me. I was not afraid of falling and I slowly pulled myself up, until I had reached

First attempt at climbing to the crow's nest

about half way. Then I said to Cyril 'I think this old lady has had enough'. He said 'That's fine. Take your time, get your breath and go down when you are ready'. No one had made me feel a nuisance or stupid. When I got down, Marco, the engineer, said 'Well how do you feel about that, Sheila?' I said 'Well, I tried, Marco, I can do no more'. He then said 'Sheila, to have tried and failed is a success, to have failed to try is a failure'. I thought that was great. Later on that day Dr Alan, who was on our watch, said 'Sheila, this afternoon you made me cry'. I said 'Alan, what on earth did I do to make you cry?' He replied 'Sheila, I have never been up the mast before, and I was terrified, and I looked down and there you were pulling yourself up and having to cope with your disabilities. It just made me feel so ashamed'. I just gave him a big hug for admitting how terrified he was.

Navigating

When leaving Fuerteventura one afternoon, our watch was on duty and I was called to the helm. Everyone else was pulling in the fenders and ropes. Then the gangplank had to be pulled on board which was a mammoth task. Marco, the engineer, the captain and myself were on the bridge with the captain viewing the world through his binoculars. The *Lord Nelson* ventured slowly forwards on engine power, which Marco was controlling. The captain said 'Keep at 90°'. I said nothing. The Captain then shouted 'What did I say?' 'Keep her at 90°, Sir'. Marco turned round to me and said 'Don't forget to repeat the Captain's instructions loudly and repeat them again loudly once you have arrived there and say, Sir'. So off the captain and Marco went to supervise the sails, leaving Sheila alone. I was now on my own. The sails were up, and the wind was beginning to take control, and I quickly discovered that I was well off course. I said to myself 'How on earth do I get back on course with the water behind me zigzagging, and me up here all alone?' But not for long! The captain came running up the steps three at a time shouting 'What the devil is going on here?' 'I have got lost, Sir'.

Navigating the correct way and with a serious face

'What did I tell you to stay at?' '90°, Sir'. 'Where are we?' 'Sir, we're at 120°, Sir'. ' Well then, how do you get back?' And only for the captain being there, I remembered how to get back. 'Are you alright now, Sheila?' And off he went, leaving me in charge once again.

Twenty-four hours after leaving Fuerteventura, we were approaching Tenerife. Our watch was on duty again, and again I was called to the helm. I thought 'What have I done to deserve this?' But you have to do as you are told. Going into port is much easier than leaving. You approach under sail, then the sails are released, and finally the engine takes over. So I repeated the orders loudly, and added 'Sir', as ordered. When we were successfully moored the captain said 'That was great, Sheila, thank you'.

'Happy Hour' is when the ship is cleaned from top to bottom. At the first 'Happy Hour', our watch was cleaning below decks. The first tasks organised are those for the disabled members and so Paul, on our watch, who has cerebral palsy, was sent to the laundry in his wheelchair, to separate towels and sheets. Then I was the next of the disabled group, so I was told to clean all the mirrors. Thankfully there was always something for me to hold onto when the ship was moving. The other jobs were shared by the able-bodied crew. There was always plenty to do - washing all the tables and benches, polishing all the woodwork, cleaning out all the toilets, and shining with Brasso any brass on the floor and walls. The cabins were then hoovered and mopped and any luggage or clothing in the sleeping areas was thrown on to the bunks. The next day our watch was on deck which was to be scrubbed. Paul and I were told to clean the portholes with newspaper and vinegar. This seems a bit odd but it does work, for I remember my Granny doing it that way. The decks were hosed down, and so was everyone else! After 'Happy Hour' it was time for smokoo, our tea and coffee break.

My next task was mess duty. I felt I could cope with this. Cleaning the tables, wiping the jelly type mats, and laying the table was fine. I was put to work in the top mess which was for the permanent crew. It was a smaller area and that suited me.

The crew were expected to scrape their own plates into a bucket and then put their plates into another bucket of hot soapy water before I put them into the dishwasher. Water also had to be recycled. The chat and craic from the permanent crew was great, as you can imagine. Cyril was there, the chap who had helped me up the mast the day before. When he arrived with his plate, I said 'Cyril, you helped me yesterday, so I will help you now and clean your plate. Can I get you anything from the bar?' So I really did look after Cyril. When the captain finished his meal, he plonked his plate down beside me. I looked at him, and then looked at his plate. I repeated this. All went quiet in the mess. I picked up the captain's plate and said 'I've got a message Sir – yesterday you saved all our lives, and the *Lord Nelson*, when you came up on to the bridge shouting up at me, so I will clean your plate, captain, Sir!' After a moment's silence, the crew all roared with laughter.

Later that day, the wind got up and the *Lord Nelson* was rocking and rolling, and it was also time for the evening meal which was spaghetti Bolognese. At mealtime you had to eat what you were given. Cyril came in holding two plates of dinner and said 'Spaghetti Bolognese for everyone.' As the ship rolled around, Cyril was, of course, serving the captain first, when, horror of horrors, two plates of very hot dinner landed on the captain's lap. As he was jumping up and down, trying to get the meal off his trousers, everyone else was falling about laughing. I was so pleased that it was Cyril, and not me, who had caused the spill. Who would have believed that it had been just an accident, if it had been me?

When we were on watch, we were on the bridge. We all took it in turns to navigate and when out at sea, even the most disabled, like Paul, with his cerebral palsy, could take the helm, with our watch leader beside him. The rest of us would be observing, watching for other vessels, or floating objects, and sometimes for dolphins, and notifying the officer on watch. We recorded the weather in the chart room every hour as well as the conditions of the sea and the water temperature. Even around the Canary Islands, where the temperature was around 70°F, it could be cool enough at night during our four-hour watch. At night the bunks were checked every half hour in bad weather to ensure that everyone was using their PVC heel pads, in case someone should fall out.

When we were in Puerto Cruz, I was on watch with our watch leader, Dr Ian. He was doing his rounds at 2am when most of the others were ashore, making merry. I heard Kathy, in her wheelchair, and her buddy coming along the quay. The tide had gone out and the gangplank was well off the ground. So in order to help, I went down the plank, and that made it touch the ground. Kathy and her buddy got onto the plank, which, of course, was very steep. With a great deal of pushing and with Kathy herself trying to help, her wheelchair tipped backwards.

And so with a great deal of giggling and laughing, and Kathy holding onto the rails, she eventually did get aboard. No sooner was Kathy aboard when Mike arrived in his wheelchair, with his buddy. Mike said 'No problem, I have just seen what happened to Kathy, so, in order to prevent another fiasco, I will get out of my wheelchair'. This he did, but the angle was too steep for his disabled feet to manage, even with holding on to the rails. So Mike, who wears callipers, fell forward onto his face. His buddy and his wheelchair were behind him and that didn't help. I ran off to the galley where two of the crew were drinking coffee, and they immediately came to my assistance. With plenty of laughing and pulling and shoving everyone decided Mike could not stand at that angle, so he got pulled up by his arms. When his wheelchair arrived, Mike was shoved into it. This enabled him to release his callipers, so that he could bend his legs. When the watch leader returned, he said 'All quiet, Sheila?' I said nothing. The things that happen when Sheila is in charge!

The Wheelies and the Wobblies

When we were in port and the weather was good, all the disabled crew members were able to get up to the crow's nest. The main mast was roped up to enable the wheelchairs to reach the crow's nest. There were five wheelchairs, and they took it in turns, and had plenty of time to enjoy the experience. The foremast was used for the wobblies who were fully harnessed and roped. They

After great difficulty I finally made it!

could be blind, deaf, epileptic, suffer from learning disabilities, or be physically disabled. The crew then said to me 'All the way, this time, Sheila'. So off I went again but it was no easier the second time round. I reached the last five steps which are angled out, so as to get into the crow's nest. Cyril was with me again, and I said 'Cyril, with my disabled hand, I will not be able to take my weight backwards'. So he asked the boys holding the rope to help. This they did, but I still had to deal with the angle and pull myself up into the crow's nest. Once I had arrived, all the crew clapped and cheered. I wondered what all the fuss was about. Once in the crow's nest there were others who were disabled, had poor sight, were epileptic, were hard of hearing or were suffering from learning disabilities. I was the only one who was physically disabled. We had only been together for thirty-six hours, and I had not appreciated this before, but the other folk had. This just proved that we were all working together, and understanding and caring for each other in a way I have never come across before. They had all given me as much help as I needed at every stage of the way to enable me to succeed and get into the crow's nest. I waved and acknowledged the crew down below, just as the Queen Mother would have done. After resting I was just hoping that getting down over that ledge would be a bit easier.

This was another example of everyone being able to achieve everything. The most disabled in wheelchairs had been hoisted

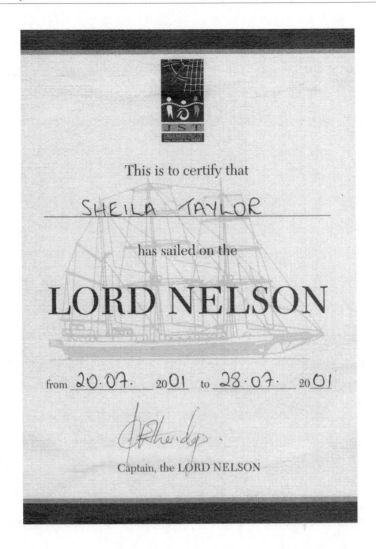

This is to certify that

SHEILA TAYLOR

has sailed on the

LORD NELSON

from 20·07· 2001 to 28·07· 2001

Captain, the LORD NELSON

up to the crow's nest and even I was able to get there myself and without my wheelchair.

I did make it. I did navigate. I did get up to the crow's nest. I did become the captain's mate – at the helm of course! All these ambitions I had achieved.

My time and experiences on the *Lord Nelson* were unforgettable. I truly appreciated and valued the total care given by all the crew members who, year after year, book and pay for a holiday, knowing that they are going to be living and working with the disabled. And nor should I forget that whenever I went ashore, the two doctors from my watch were always with me.

I often think of everyone who was involved – the permanent crew, the voluntary crew, the able-bodied, and the disabled, all of us, regardless of age, all tirelessly working together – with ropes, the wind and the wet and, lest we forget, the lack of sleep and lack of privacy.

Yet it was all a total joy – the quiet days, the warmth of the sun, the companionship, the dolphins jumping and diving alongside us, and never forgetting the beautiful sunrises and sunsets.

The horizon was our universe. We surely were travelling together with guidance from above.

Six

Cuba

My son, Mark, who is Canadian, agreed to go with me to Cuba. This was in July 2006. At Varadaro airport, Havana, he was asked about my medication. Mark asked me if I had a prescription. I told him that when I am given a prescription, I give it to the pharmacist who then gives me my medication. So I said 'No, I do not have a prescription'. The customs officer then replied with the official line to say that if anyone arrives without a prescription, then the medication has to be thrown away. Mark explained that I was ill and I did require my medication and I was let through. That was the first time that I ever had any problems with medication so I now make sure to travel with a prescription, which the pharmacist is happy to provide.

Our hotel was near the sea, and the lifeguard watched me as I walked with difficulty into the sea each day. His name was Stefan and he started talking to us, and then asked us if we would like him to take us into Havana. We asked him how much it would cost. He said that he would have to hire a car in our name, as visitors were not permitted to drive their old American cars. We asked another couple to join us, and they agreed to come along. Stefan told us he was ours for the day. The other couple wanted to see Hemingway's Bar, and I wanted to see the Hotel Nacional de Cuba. Stefan then took us to see a single room cigar factory whose owner is in the Guinness book of records, having made the longest cigar, which was 24 feet long. It was on show, up high, all around the room. I bought Mark the cigar the man was rolling on his thighs that morning. The upper class luxury coach trips, which cost £80 per person, would certainly not have seen this. We were taken to a superb

The cigar factory in Havana with the owner who made the longest ever cigar

Two old American Cadillacs on a Havana street

out-of-the-way Cuban restaurant for lunch. We invited Stefan to join us but he said he would stay with the car, but we insisted and he came. When the bill came we split it between the two couples, so that Stefan would not have to pay although I thought that he may have been a bit concerned about this. Havana was just full of well-preserved American Cadillacs. Only military and tourist vehicles are permitted to be imported into Cuba; no Cuban homes have electricity nor do they have refrigerators, washing machines or vacuum cleaners.

I wanted to go on an off-road jeep ride. Our courier said they did not sell these. However I told him I wanted to go, and if I couldn't get the tickets from him, then I would get them from the Cuban Tourist desk – which I did. Mark and I were picked

| A statue of Christ | Daydreaming about swimming with dolphins |

up by a jeep, and taken to meet the rest of our group. There were only three jeeps with Germans in one and Japanese in the other. Because of my wheelchair Mark and I went with the leader. Off the main roads Cuba is a beautiful island. Many folk live in wooden shacks and some in little houses made of concrete blocks. They have no running water or electricity. Much of their food is subsidised, such as rice and bread, although their fruit and vegetables come from the land.

Our first stop was at a cave and we all went in. The cave was very deep with stalagmites and stalactites and there was a deep pool. Everyone stripped off, dived in and were amazed at how warm the water was. It was so unexpected. Afterwards I sat in at the bar and enjoyed a beer.

With Albert, my snorkelling mentor – both of us have white hair!

The next stop was at a volcanic stone beach. At the side of the road there were five men in wet suits and we were told that we were going snorkelling. Now can this old lady snorkel? I cannot wear flippers; my feet don't work and it was very, very difficult trying to climb over those volcanic stones to let me get into the sea. My guide was Albert who was a bit older than the other lads and he just said to me 'You belong to me today, we both have white hair'. He helped me, and after a long fight I succeeded getting into the water. I had to wear my sandals to help protect my feet from the stones. Once in the water, Albert held my hand and we were off. He left me, and dived down to pick up things of interest, including a starfish. He had a plastic bottle tucked into his trunks which he got out and fed the fish. He dived down to pick up a shell that was pink and curled over and when we looked, we saw that there were fish inside. It was very heavy and when he handed it to me, I nearly sank. We did giggle. By this time the other boys were out. I found it difficult trying to get out as I had no crutch as the stones were so rough. When I did make it, Albert said 'Sheila, when I first met you, I thought, oh, this is going to be hard work. But once you were in the water, you were great!' It was so good to hear Albert say that. When you are less-able you know you are hard work and you are a problem. After all, he did not have to be such fun!

We went on and stopped at a ranch, miles from anywhere. It was away up in the mountains. After lunch we were to have gone horse riding, but then the heavens opened, so we decided to call it a day. By now it was 3.30pm, and we were a long way from home. On our way back, one of the jeeps got stuck in the mud. The driver kept over-revving, which did not help. Eventually a local farmer brought his horse and, with his western saddle, he tied a rope to the jeep and got it out of the mud. We all arrived home after a very exciting, albeit exceedingly rough, off-road jeep ride. I could see why the courier was not happy about us going. Of course we had no idea what to expect, but both of us were delighted with our totally thrilling day.

There were eight of us wanting to swim with the dolphins. We were all nationalities and I was the only one in a wheelchair.

There were four dolphins in this very wide tidal river and we were told by the lady on the pier to spread out in a line. The dolphins worked in pairs, and came up in turns and kissed us all on the cheek. The second activity was that each dolphin approached a swimmer upside down so that you could tickle or stroke his tummy. Next the dolphins worked in pairs for us to hold onto their fins and we were towed along at quite a speed. Then the swimmers had to lie on the water with our arms and legs out, like a star. The dolphins came in pairs to find our feet, push us fast by our feet, and then faster until eventually they tossed us up into the air.

Finally the dolphins came to me. They tried my feet, but as I can't point them, they knew something wasn't right, and so they went back to the lady at the pier. She asked me what was wrong. I told her my feet were disabled. She said that was fine, and sent the dolphins back to me, just to be taken for a ride

holding onto both their fins. I am glad I did have a go. After all, I may never have the opportunity to swim with dolphins again.

Somebody loves me!

Seven

Lapland

One day in 2007, when being bathed, I said I needed someone to accompany me on holiday. Geolin, my carer, said that she would be happy to go on holiday with me so I asked her if she wanted to go to the heat or to the cold. She said she didn't mind so we looked on the internet and chose a Discover the World tour travelling away over the Arctic Circle to Lapland. And so we booked a week's stay at Yllas in Finland.

Our hotel at Yllas was at the base of the highest fell in Finland and is one of the most popular skiing resorts in the country. In Lapland all the lakes freeze over from November until May. There are no birds or insects and all is quiet because there is no water. There isn't much traffic and any there is drives very quietly because the roads are always covered in snow. On our first day our courier came for us and took us in her car to a large warehouse to kit us out in our thermal gear. There were rows and rows of all-in-one-zip-up-the-front clothing. The boots were made of black rubber with a corrugated part around the ankles to ease movement. You wore as many pairs of socks as you wanted and tried to find boots that suited you. Finally we were all provided with helmets.

Our first activity was at the reindeer farm and there were three sleighs set out and ready for us. It was difficult to get me low enough into the sleigh as it was only a couple of inches off the snow but, once in, I had a lovely reindeer skin to sit on. The sleighs were all hand made from local trees and the reins were made of rope. The farmer set off first into the forest, followed by Geolin and myself. All was quiet. Then my reindeer decided he wanted a picnic so he stopped and nosed through the soft snow, and started to nibble at the moss on the trees – by which time the others had long gone. I wiggled my reins and said to the reindeer 'It isn't teatime and you'll have to get a move on'. He was not impressed. He turned round and gave me a superior look as if to say 'Who do you think is in charge of this sleigh, because it certainly isn't you, old lady?' So I had to wait. Eventually he decided he ought to catch up with the others, so off he galloped. His feet are made to spread out when he is on the snow, so as to stop him sinking. So as he galloped along his hoofs picked up a lot of snow which covered me from head to toe. Off we went through the forest, round the trees, this way and that. He seemed to know where he was going and all I had to do was

Aboard my sleigh and looking comfortable

hang on for dear life, to stay on board. We eventually caught up with the others just before we got back to the farm. Needless to say, I was the only one covered in snow. It had been so exciting. Then came the struggle to get me out of the sleigh. When you are disabled there is no point in being shy or embarrassed and so, if and when you need help, accept it in the best way possible.

The farmer took the sleighs off the reindeers and fed them. Our courier was still around and she interpreted for us. The farmer asked us if we would like to go into his wigwam. Geolin and I just looked at one another, with our mouths wide open. Neither of us had been in a wigwam before so we very carefully, me with my crutch, walked through the soft snow and entered what turned out to be quite a large wigwam. It was made of

Inside the reindeer farmer's wigwam

many thin spruce trees, and covered with reindeer skin. The trees were held together at the top with rope, and there was a fire in the middle. Obviously the smoke went through the hole in the top. Inside there were skin covered wooden benches and so we sat down. There was an old fashioned kettle on the fire. We were asked if we would like tea or coffee or local berry juice. We both plumped for the local berry juice which was served in beautiful hand made wooden cups. We asked the farmer about his life in such an isolated place. He told us that he bred his own reindeer which lived about twenty years. Wild reindeers were culled to control their numbers, and he informed us that there were more reindeer in Finland than people. Our courier then took us back to our hotel. Geolin and I were so thrilled with our day's activities in temperatures as low as -8°C, although we hadn't felt the cold which just proved that our thermal outfits had been doing their job.

Snowmobile safari

Geolin and I were delighted to discover that there were just the two of us with the Discover the World tour. Our courier then took us in her car to the side of a frozen lake where there were two young men, who spoke perfect English, and four snowmobiles. Once they saw that I was disabled they asked if I was going to drive. I said 'Yes'. They showed us the accelerator on the right of the handlebar and the brake on the left and advised that we should not do more than 30mph. So we mounted these very wide vehicles, and started off with one lad in front, then Geolin followed by me, and then the other lad at the rear. We started out over the lake. Unfortunately I found that every bump we

Ready to make tracks

went over meant that the thick ski glove on my right hand kept slipping off, which meant that I slowed down. After a while the lad behind me asked if I was all right. I explained the problem I was having with my right hand being disabled and hard to control, but that I was happy to keep going. We then approached the forest so, as you can imagine, we were in and out of the trees and jumping the jumps which there was no way of avoiding. But it was all so exciting, all white and in the beautiful sunshine.

After an hour and a half we stopped and went into a restaurant – in the middle of nowhere. They had to pull me off my snowmobile first, and let me stand up. One and a half hours with legs outstretched was difficult to cope with and, because I only have one hand that moves properly, Geolin had to take my helmet off. Once in the restaurant I needed her to unzip my all-in-one thermal suit so that I could visit the toilet. Then I sat down at the table and ordered reindeer meat which did not have a very distinctive flavour but tasted a bit like lamb. We started talking to the boys, and they told us that they had helped build the nearby ice hotel. They had to wait until the ice on the lake was exactly two feet thick and then it had to be cut into squares in order to build the hotel. They said it took about ten of them three weeks to build the basic hotel which only consisted of ice, since nothing else was permitted. The carvings, tables, and sculptures were only added afterwards.

When it was time for the return trip I asked if I could be a pillion passenger. I was tired and ached from sitting awkwardly for so long that morning. The boys said 'No problem'. They just could not believe that I had had the courage to ride the snowmobile on my own that morning with my disabilities.

The fabulous Ice Hotel

Geolin and I were so pleased that we belonged to such a small group, because you can imagine that if I had been one of twenty other riders, I would have been a nuisance every time my hand had slipped off the accelerator. We would also have missed the experience of finding out about the ice hotel.

Ice Hotel

Geolin and I then went to visit the Ice Hotel, which we knew was only made of ice. The temperature inside was -8°C, the same as outside. It was built in a Spanish style with archways and all white. There were no doors, only reindeer skins to provide privacy. The dining room consisted of ice tables and ice bench seats, but I don't think anyone sat down, except maybe to appreciate the wall sculptures. The beds were blocks of ice. The corridors were wide with two particularly magnificent carvings, one of a vodka bottle that reached the ceiling, and the other of a large bear standing on his back legs. The carvings on the walls were mostly of landscapes and dolphins.

You pay £100 to stay the night. You get your arctic type sleeping bag that covers your head and, of course, your ears. You undress if you so desire, but I would think that removing your boots, if you really wanted to, would be as much as most people would accomplish. You cannot read because lights of any kind give off heat and you cannot have any water, because this would turn to ice. You cannot have a pee because this too would turn to ice, and for this reason there is no restroom. If you require any of these luxuries, you cross the road to the tourist hotel. You are able to use the hotel lounge chairs and settees if you really cannot cope with your rather expensive night in the ice hotel. Most guests have a torch, and the light from the hotel and restaurant outside helps to illuminate the ice hotel.

Dog Sleigh

We were taken to the husky farm, and this was the first time Geolin and I were aware that there were other holiday makers, including a group of fourteen from Thomas Cook. We were introduced to the sleighs which were hand made with a high back. The sides of the sleighs were quite narrow and came round

The dog sleigh with our hard working huskies

the back. You stand on these, and hold on to the back rail. There was a higher piece of wood which was the brake. All the dogs want to do is race off and we have no physical control of the dogs, other than the brakes. The dogs work as a team, and they decide who the leader is. There was one dog with a cut lip that had once been the leader, but now a younger husky had taken over.

When they go round a corner you go with it like riding a motorbike. I decided that I would not be able to control the sleigh, so I asked if I could go as a passenger. Luckily I was put with the 'back stop' driver, so I could see all that was going on, and how the others coped when they fell off.

They never told you that if you fell off, your dogs just ran on, and you had to run, knee deep in snow, to catch them up. Thank goodness I had enough sense to say I just wanted to be a passenger. Our ride covered fifteen kilometres, across lakes and in and out of forests. Yes, it was a rough ride, and I had to hold on tight. It was a beautiful sunny day and the trees were thick with lovely soft snow. This was the first time that I felt cold, sitting on a reindeer skin only a couple of inches above the snow, but at least I had another skin on my lap. But I suppose I was sitting there doing nothing, just watching those who fell off trying to catch their dogs!

The Northern Lights

The Northern Lights appear when the solar wind particles collide with the molecules in the earth's atmosphere. There were some

The Northern Lights – the photos don't do it justice

nights when we just saw green that could have been clouds, but on another night we saw a multi-coloured fusion that stretched across the sky. Many people went outside the hotel and lay on their backs recording this extraordinary sight.

We enjoyed our experiences in Lapland and our hotel was well provided for. On our one free day Geolin pushed me down to the nearby village, where they had stores and tourist souvenirs for sale. After having a cup of tea and local cake, we caught a taxi back. I was always kind to Geolin, not wanting to wear her out, as we didn't know what would be expected of us the next day.

Eight
The Tall Ships race

It was suggested, in July 2001, that I should see if I would be able to take part in the Tall Ships race on the *Lord Nelson*. Each year between 80 and 130 sail training vessels, carrying as many as 3000 young trainees, participate in what was known in the year I took part as the Cutty Sark Tall Ships race. Some of the trainees were at the beginning of their careers as professional sailors, but most, like me, were enjoying a once-in-a-lifetime experience of life at sea in a vessel propelled by the wind. The vessels ranged from small 40ft yachts to full size square-riggers built in bygone days and now adapted for cadet sailing. The race was for eighteen to twenty-five year olds but, as the *Lord Nelson* catered for the disabled and had a permanent crew, 25% of the crew was permitted to be over twenty-five years of age. The two largest sailing ships were the *Sedov*, a Russian boat with

Our watch on the Lord Nelson

250 cadets, and the *Dar Mlodziezy*, a Polish boat, also with 250 cadets on board.

When receiving my travelling instructions I noted that I was leaving Gatwick airport at about 2am, and the return flight was also at a similar time. I phoned Monarch Airlines to ask why. I reassured them that I was not complaining but was curious about the very early flight times. After checking the flights they came back to me and said 'Are you in the Tall Ships race?' I told them that I was and then they were able to tell me that this was the only time they could give us a slot to fly, because the flight was completely booked for Tall Ships crew.

Also in my travelling instructions there was a map of Bergen, showing the harbour mooring plan. It made me realise all the work and planning that was required to decide which boats go where. The larger ones had to be against a pier, and the smaller ones along side each other. So every one had to moor at the precise position as instructed by the harbour authorities.

The *Lord Nelson* had a totally different crew from my previous trip with them. This time everyone came on their own and the Jubilee Sailing Trust had to pair up each disabled crew member with a buddy. Because many of the crew were changing in Alesund, they had to allow the first day for all crew to understand the running of the ship, just as before – learning to man the sails, understanding your watch and your watch leader and their instructions. Again wet gear had only to be worn on deck, because it was so noisy. Stugeron tablets were available on each deck to help control seasickness and, if you were sick, you were required to clean up after yourself. No alarm clocks were allowed with the next watch being woken up by the watch on duty. Safety harnesses were to be worn by all crew on deck, which enabled you to clip onto a metal ring which was very necessary in rough weather. We were now in the North Sea.

When preparing to leave port, each ship had to wait until told when to leave. The *Shabab Oman* was moored near us and all their musicians were up on deck playing their eastern music with bagpipes and drums, waving to each ship as it passed on its way out of the harbour and getting ready to join in the Parade of the Sails. It really was a magical atmosphere.

The Parade of the Sails and the martial music

When leaving port all ships were asked to go under sail – the Parade of the Sails. This was a magnificent sight with each ship going when directed. It was a very tricky exercise for our captain, especially with so many small boats coming out to see us, for it does take a sailing ship time to alter course in an effort to avoid sightseers who just want to soak up the atmosphere. The Parade of the Sails is a way of saying 'Thank you' to the port authorities who had entertained so many young crew over the previous three or four days. They had willingly spent a great deal of money and time entertaining hundreds of young people, with bands and dance music, fast food for the ever hungry and offering different sports, such as football, for them. And to add to all this, they had provided coaches for those who wanted to go sightseeing. And finally all the ships had to get themselves into the correct position to start the next leg of the race.

Our next port of call was Flora. When in port all crews were expected to partake in the Parade of the Crews and so we took part as expected. There were five of us in wheelchairs, and I was asked to carry the banner of the *Lord Nelson*. This reminded me of the Olympics when all teams march around the arena behind their national banners. As the large Russian crew from the *Sedov* passed by, we were waiting in a side street ready to join the parade. Just then the crew from the *Shabab Oman* passed along and they spotted us. Their musicians with their bagpipes and drums left the rest of their crew members, stopped playing and joined together dancing and clapping all around us. They kissed and hugged those of us in wheelchairs, before eventually allowing the parade to continue. This brought tears to my eyes. But I continued to carry the banner as instructed.

As we were approaching the port of Bergen, there was a battleship which was firing salvoes to welcome us. As always we had to moor in the exact place and, to assist us, we picked up a pilot who guided us in by giving out his orders. Once moored, we made sure that everything was in perfect order and the crew were allowed to go ashore. The watch on duty was told by the watch leader which two of us were to remain, as there always had to be some permanent crew on board. On the first day some local Norwegians provided our evening meal. A local television camera crew then came on board and asked me if I had enjoyed their meal. I said that I had, and then he asked me if I knew what it was. Imagine being asked this question on television, when I hadn't a clue. I said 'I realised it was a stew with tomatoes and fish'. He then asked if I knew which fish, which of course I didn't. He went on to explain that, because of their weather, they had to smoke and preserve their catches so that it would last the winter months. So we live and learn. And after all that he didn't even tell me what kind of fish it was. The interview, with yours truly, appeared on television that evening.

The Bergen Viking Ships race was due to take place the next day so I made my way down to the pier to join the crew

Our Viking boat

Found myself a fella!

who were preparing to participate in the race. Each ship has ten rowers sitting on five bench seats with a Viking assigned to steer. No doubt hoping to prevent any accidents from Tall Ship crews, the *Lord Nelson* was carefully sorting out its crew. Only two boats raced at a time, and it was against the clock. Then I told the first mate, Claire, that I was going. How I'd manage, I wasn't quite sure. On hearing this, two other wheelchair girls, both called Fiona, declared 'If Sheila is going, so are we'. This was surely going to present a bit of a problem for the crew. There certainly is far more to being a member of the permanent crew of the *Lord Nelson* than just giving out orders to the voluntary crew, and making sure they do as they are told. When it was time for the *Lord Nelson* to board its crew onto the Viking boat, a wheelchair friendly toilet had to be found. After this the two Fionas were carried along on canvas seats provided by the Jubilee Sailing Trust. I was then taken to the pier and, with supervision from below, managed to get on board the long boat. I decided I would rather sit at the back with the Viking. Each pair of rowers was then provided with an oar. The two Fionas sat squeezed in the middle on their two seats which meant they could help as much as they felt able.

I was at the back with no particular job, so once everyone was settled, I shouted 'I'm in charge', and they all had to do as they were told. The two lads in front of me had good timing as I called out 'Up heave'. They all got the message and their timing and speed were quite good. When we reached the finishing line, the Viking said 'Stop and turn round'. I shouted at our Viking 'I'm in charge of this ship and we'll keep going until I tell you to stop. We're setting course for Scotland across the North Sea. It has been done before!'

When we arrived back at the pier, many people shouted and cheered, because we were all from the *Lord Nelson*, and three of us were in wheelchairs. All three of us were so thrilled that we had been able to take part in the race. The *Lord Nelson* had turned up trumps again. Thank you one and all.

We all returned home to Gatwick. The crew was changing again to partake in the long five-day sea journey race to Esbjerg in Denmark.

Deciding the winner of this race is a very involved affair which includes, amongst other matters, the size of the ship. I was so pleased to see on the internet that all the captains, having seen all that their crew had done to promote international friendship and understanding, had voted the *Shabab Oman* the winner and they were accordingly awarded the Cutty Sark Trophy.

Our smiling and enthusiastic crew members – taken at sea

Nine

Never be alone at Christmas. The Salvation Army is there for everyone.

On Christmas Eve 2008 I went to the parish church of St Philip and St James in Holywood. On my way out the vicar said 'See you tomorrow, Sheila'. I replied 'No you won't'. So he asked why. I told him that, as I was on my own, I was going to spend Christmas Day with the Salvation Army. He asked if I had been before and when I said 'No', he asked me to write and let him know how I had got on.

So, as promised, I sent the vicar a letter telling him about my first Christmas Day at the Salvation Army Temple on the Cregagh Road in Belfast. They had drivers who went down the Ards Peninsula to collect people but I was able to drive myself there. I really did not know what to expect. How many people there would be and what type of people would be happy to spend Christmas with the Salvation Army. It was snowing when I arrived and I went in and was made most welcome. First of all they had a service which was taken by the major and her husband. On everyone's seat was a carol praise sheet and on many of the sheets there was a little number and a name. Before the service started Major Yvonne said there was going to be an unrehearsed nativity play. She then called out names and numbers and people were asked to respond, to ensure that all the parts were taken. Anyone not wanting to take part was asked to hand over their sheet to someone else. I got the part of an ox and although I have forgotten what I had to say, I do remember that my words were followed by three 'moos!' For an 'instant unrehearsed nativity play', it worked very well. When my 'moos' were delivered, all the Salvation Army boys joined in and this made everyone laugh. The service itself was mainly hymns and carols and they also said the Lord's Prayer. There were around thirty to forty people in the congregation.

After the service we went into the reception hall where there were plenty of seats. There we were offered tea and coffee and mince pies. I only then realised there were three other folk from Bayview whom I knew and so we asked if we could sit together. I didn't know what the dining arrangements would be like but when we were invited into the dining room I saw that there were tables each set for six. So the four of us sat together with a chap in a wheelchair, and a Salvation Army officer at the end of our table. Altogether there were only about thirty-six of us although I think I was certainly expecting more. The company was mixed with some who probably lived in hostels, and of course, others who would have lived alone. We had a very good lunch. Sammy Wilson, a former Lord Mayor of Belfast, was there. It seems that one year he carved the turkey and another year he did the washing up. In the afternoon there was entertainment put on by any of us who wanted to sing and by the children of the Salvation Army. We left for home around 4 o'clock, with a lovely bag of Christmas presents.

Just before leaving I called Major Yvonne over and said to her, 'You asked your children at the service what they had received for Christmas but I hope you all realise that the greatest gift that we have all received today was being able to come here and share your Christmas lunch'. She replied by saying that was always their only wish to know that all of us had been able to leave our homes and come and share Christmas together with them.

I looked for somewhere to put some money but as there were no boxes in the church or in the reception area, I went up and found the major's Bible and left something there. You don't want to be taking all the time, and forgetting to give.

All in all it was a super day. I knew I had been lucky finding people I knew with whom to share a table but I was also glad that I had found the Salvation Army and, as a consequence, you don't need to feel you are being a burden on anyone. And I was glad to know that the Salvation Army officers have Boxing Day off when they can celebrate their own Christmas Day with their friends and families.

So you need never be alone on Christmas Day.

Ten

Canada and Alaska

How not to start a holiday!

Canada

I left my flat in Holywood one morning early in June 2011 at 5.30am by taxi to catch the 7am flight to Gatwick from Belfast City airport. As we were nearing Gatwick, fog descended and we started to go round and round. The hands on the clock also went round and round. When we eventually landed and my wheelchair had arrived, I said to the young porter 'I hate to tell you, but my flight for Calgary leaves in an hour'. He said 'Right, I'll leave you here and get your luggage and I'll tell the gate you are here'. When he returned he said that if we were not there an hour before take off – tough. I responded by saying, 'Right, what are you going to do with me now? You have an old lady in a wheelchair with no ticket, and you have to hand her over to someone'. He said he would go with me to the Canadian Affairs desk. So off we went, and I told them that I had missed the flight because of the fog. Then I was told that they didn't have another flight to Calgary for three days. I told him that my granddaughter was waiting for me in Calgary, but he insisted that he was unable to get me there. The conversation was by now becoming a little heated and I said, 'Well, get me anywhere in Canada and I will get to Calgary myself'. He checked his schedules and told me he could get me to Vancouver that afternoon. The flight would leave in three hours time. He assured me that there was a seat available for me, and handed me the phone in order that I could give my Visa card information to pay for my ticket. Then my Visa card refused payment and I had no other credit card with me at that time. (I do now!) The price for the one-way ticket was £530, because it was needed that day. I did, however, have my direct debit card, but that only had my monthly pocket money. Were they able to pay £530? I tried and luckily they did. So I got my ticket and was sent round to departure. My porter was now able to hand me over. I phoned the Visa card people and asked what they were playing at. I told them that I was in Gatwick, had missed my flight because of fog and had been refused credit on my card when I knew I had plenty of money available. They checked my details and said my address was not exactly as they had it on their computer. (So I now have cut out the address and information which I receive with my bills and keep this with me so that this doesn't happen again). I told him I was going to Canada, and I would need to use this credit card, and I certainly hoped that I wouldn't be refused money again. He assured me that this would not happen and I could continue to use the card in shops, hotels and at ATMs.

The next thing I had to do was contact my granddaughter, Kathryn. She lived in Canada, and had no paper work, and possibly no money, because grandmother had everything. I used the airport computer, with my hopefully now useable Visa card, but every time I started to type, I was asked 'Do you want to play bingo?' Each time I said 'No, I didn't want to play bingo'. Eventually I was able to send a quick email to Kathryn, 'Missed plane, stay with Travelsphere, I will find you'. Luckily Kathryn received my email, went to Travelsphere, introduced herself and said grandma had all the paperwork. They allowed her to travel on the coach and off they went from Calgary to Banff, about eighty miles away. Luckily for Kathryn a mother and father with a girl about Kathryn's age had seen her walking around Banff on her own later on that evening and they kindly invited her to join them for a meal.

I eventually arrived in Vancouver and then took an internal flight to Calgary. Upon arrival in Calgary I said to a porter that I needed to get a taxi to take me to Banff and could he please take me to an ATM, as I knew I would probably need around $200 for the fairly long journey. He obliged, I withdrew my money and then went along to find the cheapest taxi to Banff. The driver turned out to be a Pakistani and I sat in the front with him, and asked him if he went this way often. He replied that he had never been to Banff before – and I told him I had never been there either. We did have a laugh! His sat-nav got us there about 3am, by which time I had been travelling well over twenty-seven hours. I was tired out as you can imagine. At the hotel I got out of the taxi, set up my wheelchair and put my bag on my lap. As I approached the desk I noticed two beautifully attired youngsters, possibly from a wedding party, chatting up the porter. I interrupted them and informed the porter that I was Sheila Taylor, that I was with Travelsphere, and that I wanted my key now! The key was thrust into my hand and I went over to the lift. But when I got to the bedroom door I could not open it because of my disabled hand. And then, lo and behold, Kathryn opened the door and said 'Oh hello, Grandma', to which I replied, 'Hello Kathryn. Go back to bed and go to sleep, and goodnight!' We did laugh.

We now needed to travel to Vancouver so we decided to cross this part of Canada by coach. It was cheaper than the train; made for a longer holiday; offered comfort stops every three or four hours and, above all, allowed us to visit lots of interesting villages and places of natural beauty. Our coach was a large 52-seater but there were only eighteen passengers on board which meant that we all got on very well and everyone was very tolerant and kind to Kathryn and me, especially the driver.

The courier told us on the first day that everyone was asked to change seats daily. That first day Kathryn and I sat well back in the coach, as I was always last on. It took me longer to get on and off because I always wanted to ensure that my wheelchair was on board. On the second day the front seat was empty when we got on, last as usual. The next day the front seat was again empty so I said in a loud voice 'Excuse me, am I permitted to sit in the front or will I get told off by the courier?' One of the men said 'Who would dare tell you off, Sheila? We kept that seat especially for you'. So I thanked them all and said 'It did not take me long to train you all, did it?' So that was how it was. They kept the front seat for Kathryn and me from then on. And when I was getting off the coach, I always had my crutch in my left hand, but needed a friendly arm to give me balance as I got down that last step and there was always someone willing to help.

On our journey we came across some wonderful sights like the world-renowned Lake Louise. Then at the end of a very narrow track we came to Lake Moraine where hikers were being attacked by a grizzly bear called 'Boo'. Therefore, for safety's sake, hikers were forbidden to use this area because man needed respect the bears' habitat. After a while things became very peaceful again, so the foresters decided to search and find

Lake Louise

Exquisite wooden scultures fashioned by local lumberjack, Peter Ryan

out why. It seemed that 'Boo' had found a mate and was now a contented family bear. Another day we ventured up a very steep, dangerous and narrow road to see the Takakkaw Falls, one of the highest waterfalls in Canada. Then we stopped off in a village called Hope where a local lumberjack called Peter Ryan had sculptures all around the area. He had started off years ago by carving an eagle with high wings out of a 12-foot high stump. The villagers were thrilled and now Hope was on the tourist map because of this skilled lumberjack. And we would not have seen all these places if we had been travelling on the train.

Alaska

After time spent touring Vancouver, Kathryn and I boarded the Holland America line ship, *ms Zuiderdam*, to go on a cruise to Alaska. There were 1,824 guests, and 800 crew. On the first day we were at sea, we quickly discovered that there were always plenty of things to do. Kathryn decided to go to dancing lessons that first afternoon and then, in the evenings, we could go to the cinema or to a live show where big bands played dance music. There was a casino open every evening and a swimming pool under a movable glass roof. If you wanted a quiet corner to read or just enjoy the view, there were plenty of these on all decks. There was one deck open for all kinds of food – everyone's taste was catered for including Indian and Chinese cuisine. Food and drinks were available twenty-four hours a day. Meals in

Kathryn, my granddaughter, and myself aboard the ms Zuiderdam

the dining room or restaurant where you were served, had set times and, when booking, you were asked if you wished to dine with your family or friends, or if you wished to mix with other guests. Kathryn and I decided that we would mix and, during the voyage, we ate with a Canadian couple and an English couple. We always had plenty to chat about.

On the evening before we had a shore trip, the timetable was slipped under our cabin door. Because the Rockies were so near, there were no coach trips but we were able to choose from helicopter or seaplane flights; trips up to a mountain top with a mountain bike ride down; deep sea fishing or a train ride on the

Yukon route railroad. These are just some of the exciting tour offers I can remember.

Juneau, the capital of Alaska, was our first port of call. Here we decided to go on a helicopter ride to view the beautiful wooden and highly painted buildings of the city and then to fly out to see the glaciers, and to return by the beautiful green forests and slopes of the Rockies.

Skagway, with its 850 all-year-round residents, was our next stop. This little city is known as the gateway to the Klondike Gold rush. We decided to venture on an unforgettable journey on the White Pass railway, built 100 years ago. We rose from sea level to 2,865 feet before reaching Fraser where the wooden buildings looked really old. There we visited a husky farm where we stopped for lunch.

Ketchikan is the salmon capital of the world, situated in the heart of the seventeen million acre Tongass National Forest. Discovery of gold and copper as well as the salmon led to the corporation of Ketchikan being founded in 1900. Kathryn and I picked up a seaplane there and we flew around viewing all the forests and the places where they mined the gold and copper. We landed on a glacier, and Kathryn ventured on to the ice. There were holes in the ice which showed deep blue water, which must have been there for many thousands of years. Everything was just so different from any of the other trips we had previously enjoyed.

Seaplanes at Ketchikan

Tongass National Park

Then we sailed past Glacier Bay which was totally covered in ice 200 years ago. The glacier used to be 4,000 feet thick and twenty miles wide but now it is in rapid retreat and scientists are hoping to learn how this is affecting climate change, taking into account, of course, the increased volume of water in the sea.

Once we arrived back in Vancouver, we realised what a wonderful experience we had enjoyed together. I could not have gone without Kathryn being there to help me in my wheelchair in order for us to take part in all the activities in which we participated. I do realise how lucky I am having these memories, and Kathryn still talks of all the excitement, luxuries and wonders of sailing around Alaska.

Eleven

Tod Mountain ranch

My elder son, Mark, is Canadian. He knows I love horses, and we as a family were lucky enough to live in Hampshire, where Mark, Paul, and I, with Shandy our dog, would go out riding for the day in the National Trust property around us, Frensham Ponds. This allowed the horses to drink, and the rest of us to enjoy our picnic with Shandy.

Mark booked for the two of us to go to Tod Mountain Ranch in British Columbia in Canada in late June 2011. Mark drove us there from his home in Ottawa and we were miles away from civilisation. Our mobile phone wouldn't work, our sat-nav was telling us where we were, when we obviously were not, and we found ourselves driving along all sorts of dirt tracks, but we did eventually arrive. At the ranch there was one main building, with one large activity room and at the end the kitchen, with the chef in charge. There was a large wooden table made of trees cut in half, which seated the sixteen horse riders, and the wranglers, whom we would know as cowboys. At the far end there were large settees and easy chairs, around a huge open log fire. At the side was a television, a DVD player and a pool table, with a darts board in the corner. A large container for beer and cold drinks was available for all, as well as wine at the table if requested. And all this was included in the price.

Our accommodation was in two berth wooden cabins, so that you never felt alone in the forest. Ours had two bedrooms, a kitchen and a bathroom. The wooden furniture, beds and wardrobes, were hand made and there was garden furniture outside. Each cabin was very secluded and out of sight of all the others.

You went out to ride as you desired, two hours in the morning or two hours in the afternoon, for example, or, if you felt like it for three, four or five hours. You just told the wranglers what you wanted to do. Some folk wanted a quieter ride and others a faster one. So you can understand how important it was to put the right rider on the right horse. As far as I was concerned, I was happy with two hours in the morning. They tried to keep you with your own horse, so that you could get to know one another. All the horses were in the corral when the time came for the ride to start. One rider mounted or dismounted at a time. As you don't know your horse, and he doesn't know you, so you needed a wrangler around just to be safe. They had plastic steps for me to get mounted. It took one of the wranglers to hold the horse's bridle, another at the side to control the saddle, and Mark with me to give me a shove when it was needed.

Once we were outside, all our hats had to be fixed to our clothing. All riders wore cowboy boots and any coats or jackets, not being worn, had to be tied by the straps provided, to the saddle. We stopped every hour or so to give the horses a breather, as the paths within the forest were very steep. This also allowed those who needed it, to go behind the trees. I always had to make sure I did not need to for, if I had dismounted, they would never have got me on again. Mark was asked if he was prepared to ride an Indian horse. It had taken them ages to train him to wear a saddle, but they had never been able to get him to accept a bridle. He used a one-rope halter. So Mark rode with the halter and the horse obeyed his hand movements on this neck without causing Mark any concern. One day we saw a black bear. He was not concerned about us, and we all went on our way. One evening, when leaving our activity room to drive to our cabin, we noticed in a field nearby a large herd of deer. I only then realised that I had not noticed any deer in the forest when we had been out on our horses.

The meals were excellent. The chef was aware that I needed a special diet, and would always ask Mark if I could eat what was on offer for, if not, he would provide an alternative.

Mark mounting his horse – notice the steps

*Sheila – the expert
horsewoman*

Our riders were all nationalities, Japanese, Australian, German, French, Canadian, American and British. At one meal one of the Japanese guests said to me 'Mark is very good bringing you on this holiday'. I replied 'Yes, I suppose he is happy to do this before I die!' Everyone laughed, but poor Mark could only say 'Mother, how can you say these things?'

I did appreciate Mark spending this time with me, and his wife being happy with this arrangement, which enabled her to spend time with her family. We all joined up together after our exciting vacation.

Twelve

Adventures for all – Disability Sports

Swimming at the Lagan Valley Leisureplex

There is so much available in Northern Ireland for those of us who, for whatever reason, are less-able. I went to Bayview Resource Centre in Bangor, and we often went to the local swimming pool where I had to teach myself to swim with my feet fused at 90°. I was invited to take part in the Disability Sports swimming championship in November 2004. I could not believe it for, although I could swim twelve lengths in the Bangor pool, I could only do it very slowly. However I was persuaded, or actually pushed, into entering this competition. And before the forms could be filled in, a teacher/instructor had to time you. I said I would do one length on my back, and so I was timed.

I drove myself down to the Lagan Valley Leisureplex in Lisburn, where I got checked in. I found the changing cubicles and, as I was putting my gear into the locker, a Downs Syndrome lad called over, 'I will be with you in a minute, mate, I'm going to the toilet'. I responded 'That's good, because you can show me where to go'. He did that, and when I came out he was waiting for me. 'Who are you swimming with?' I said 'Bayview'. He took me to the bench with the Bayview sign above it, and made sure I had a towel and a Royal Mail READY WILLING AND ABLE t-shirt. I sat down and thought – now wasn't that great, the disabled helping the disabled. If he had been an able bodied person, I would have stopped and asked where the toilets were, only to have been told – 'Over there,' with a finger pointing in their direction.

I read the programme carefully, and noticed that in the first heat of each stroke for my races there were only three competitors, while the others all had eight. Against each competitor's name was their time and they were put into heats according to their ability – which was just as well because they did have the Olympic team there as well!

When my name was called, they had a hoist ready to lower me into the pool. I should have been in the nearside lane, but I found myself in the middle one. As I was trying to get under the ropes in the pool, a wee frail girl, possibly about ten or twelve years old, was lifting the ropes up for me. Again, it was a case of the disabled helping the disabled. As I have said, I was in a heat with only three competitors, the other two being just youngsters. When the whistle sounded, off went the two youngsters. By the time they had finished, I was only half way there. But when I eventually arrived, I got a standing ovation. It must have been since I was the only grey haired old lady there. There may have been, amongst the competitors that day, one or two in their 40s, but no one, like myself, over 60. I was awarded a bronze medal, and the other two whizz kids with me received the gold and

The swimming bronze medallist

silver. The whole competition had been well thought out, and had encouraged even the most disabled to feel that they were not only welcome, but that they too could return home with their own hard earned medals.

Sailing at Craigavon, September 2005

I was invited, through Bayview Resource Centre, to take part in a sailing weekend on the lakes at Craigavon. When I arrived there were eight of us who were disabled – all lads aged under 25 plus one old grey haired granny! In order to get everyone to relax and have a good laugh, we formed pairs and headed out in a speedboat.

We were then divided into two groups and introduced to our Laser boats. Each one took the four of us, and our leader, comfortably. The weather was fair with sunny spells, although at times the wind did pick up, but this made the experience all the more exciting. We went faster and faster and had to learn to tack, and miss the boom. The leaders were kind and considerate, and told us that if we got cold, or wanted to go ashore, we were just to say so. We all went ashore for lunch, and had fun chatting about our experiences and once again these young lads were only too willing to help me get ashore.

After lunch we were told that the Mayor of Craigavon was coming down to see the sports facilities by the lakes. The photographers were there, and the Mayor, complete with his

Sailing at Craigavon

chain and all his regalia, was invited to get into one of our Laser boats to be photographed with us. He chose our boat, but would not allow us to give him a spin around the lake as he was not happy being on the water. I hope his photos turned out with a smile on his face!

I certainly enjoyed my weekend sailing on the Craigavon Lakes. The club is there for everyone, all the year round.

Water skiing

I was invited, in 2005, by Disability Sports NI to take part in a day of water skiing at the Meteor Water Ski club on Lough Henney, just south of Carryduff. (This is where Kelly Gallagher, Northern Ireland's partially sighted competitor, did her training when getting ready to represent Northern Ireland in the Paralympics). Anyway I arrived at 8.45am as requested but everywhere was locked up. Eventually another car arrived and I got out of my car and introduced myself to young Sarah, who was thirteen and in a wheelchair, and her parents. They had never been water skiing before which was a relief to know.

The gates were opened just after 9am. We went to a warehouse and I was asked what size of a wet suit I wanted. I had no idea. I just stood there and said 'this size' as I stretched out my arms. I was thrown a black rubber suit. We went over to the changing room which was a communal room with benches. Both Sarah and I were in our swimming costumes. Sarah's mother helped her dress but I could not cope on my own. The wet suit was tight with a big zip up the back and, with my disabled hands, I could not get sorted. Luckily Sarah's father was there, and yes, he dressed me!

I went down to the pier. I was offered a wide ski with a fitted boot but with my fixed feet, it did not look right for me. I was then offered a kneeling ski but, as my feet are not able to point, and my knees are not the best, this didn't seem right for me either. Then they said, 'Can you sit down?' 'Yes' I replied – 'I can sit'. So they produced a ski with a seat.

Sarah's parents then helped me on to this ski. There was a small metal frame to sit in, with a wide plastic strap under which to put your feet. Sarah's parents lowered me into the water. I called to them 'The ski is sinking, and the wet suit is not working as my bum is getting wet'. Everyone was laughing, except me. Alwyn Bingham from Disability Sports was there in his wheelchair and he said 'Sheila, it will be more than your bum that will be wet soon!'

The boat arrived, and I expected to be towed behind it, just like we see on the television. It came along with a rail out at the side which I tried to reach, but as one arm is shorter than the other, so it was not easy. They reassured me that as soon as I got moving, I would rise.

So off we went across the lake and, as I was trying to gain my confidence, my bum left the seat, the ski left me and shot off on its own. I was left hanging on the bar shouting 'Excuse me, but where has my ruddy ski gone?' I was left hanging up there just like a monkey – all white hair and black wet suit! The boat came back and asked if I could swim over to the pier. So I did swim back to the pier on my back, although not terribly quickly.

The boat collected my ski, and they asked if I wanted another go but, by then, I had decided that water skiing was not for me. However I was glad that I had had a go. I did enjoy the excitement of it all, although if Sarah's parents had not been there and willing to help me, things could have been very different.

Sarah was able to enjoy her time on a large tyre towed behind the boat. So once again there is something for everyone, regardless of ability, or disability.

A few weeks later, the vicar, Roger Elks, asked me to write about my water skiing experiences in the parish magazine. I was

Water skiing on Lough Henney

happy to do this and entitled my report 'The Wreck's Progress'. I described every gory detail of that day on, or rather, in the water and that, although I declared that I hadn't really enjoyed the adventure, I freely admitted that I was glad I had gone and had enjoyed the thrill and excitement of it all. In his remarks about my story, Roger reminded his parishioners that they all knew Sheila and knew her as 'an intrepid invalid'. He had been talking about comfort zones and how that Sheila consistently moved outside her own comfort zone. For her the pleasure of achievement far outweighed the effort and fear involved. She delighted in discovering what was possible even with her disabilities. His message concluded with the sort of words that I would regularly use – go for it! I believe that whatever I do, I am never alone.

The *Lord Rank*

Disability Sports NI asked me if I would like to spend a weekend in 2005 sailing on the *Lord Rank* which is a small sailing ship owned by the Ocean Sailing Trust moored at the Bangor Marina. The plan was that the ship would host six disabled crew members along with six able bodied ones who would act as buddies to the disabled, together with five permanent crew. When I arrived there were five lads with learning disabilities, and myself. The learning disabilities boys had their carers or a family member with them, and Sheila was on her own, and they provided a teacher from a special school who had come to see if this arrangement would be suitable for her pupils.

However, upon my arrival, I found it impossible to climb down from the pier onto the ship. There were no steps. They tried to find some mechanical method of getting me on board, searching their toolboxes and the like, but they were unsuccessful so they just, with a bit of manhandling, got me on board. Everyone had to have their own sleeping bags, pillows or duvet so it was difficult getting everyone and everything on board. Eventually we were told to get into the galley and find ourselves a bunk. I knew I had to have a bottom bunk. To get down there was a ladder against the wall and, with my disabled feet and arms, there was no way I could get down other than frontwards, on my bum and holding on with one hand as well as I could. Being an experienced lady, I got down first, landed

On board the Lord Rank*. The cabin space was very tight!*

on the first bottom bunk with my baggage, and sat tight. It was just the same as on the *Lord Nelson* – no privacy. Boys and girls had to mix and I found that I had a 45-year-old man above me and beside me, about 18 inches away, a delightful 18-year-old lad, with his buddy above him. The toilet was made of stainless steel with wooden slats on the floor. I noticed that when the ship was sailing the floor got wet with the boys splashing about. I had to dress and undress on my bed, as my arm is short, so it did not take me long to realise that t-shirt, bra and pants stay on all weekend. Thank the Lord for baby wipes and panty liners!

A rota was made out. Everyone took it in turns to do the cooking, washing up and cleaning, as well as setting the sails and navigating. The first day we sailed north. It was cold, windy and rough and I got very cold, so I just put myself to bed and read. In the evening we went ashore and visited the local pub and we did not return home to the *Lord Rank* until after midnight. The first night when we were in bed, the captain came and said 'No more talking. Lights out'. Young Jonathan beside me waved me a little good night kiss. I was so pleased and it made me feel that, although I was so much older, the others were prepared to accept me.

The second day was sunny and beautiful. All in all it was a super weekend. We all got on so well at meal times, on deck and in the pub. After we had cleaned the ship and waiting to get off, we were asked 'What was our worst experience, and what was our best?' I replied that my first shock was finding that I was expected to climb down a ladder, with two disabled feet and a disabled arm. My best experience was when Jonathan sent me a good night kiss on the first night. Some of the able bodied and permanent crew had said what a pleasure it had been to meet me and to see how well I had coped with my disabilities. I was quite pleased about that.

The Ulster Gliding Club, Bellarena – Learning to be like a seagull

As I was not provided with my angels wings as was expected after my road accident, I had to find another way to satisfy my urge to fly.

Ready to go gliding at Bellarena

Disability Sports NI recently had been presented, by the Lottery fund, with a glider specially designed for the disabled. It can take a hoist which can lift anyone in a wheelchair into the pilot's seat and it is hand controlled. The Ulster Gliding Club keeps the glider at their Bellarena airfield near Limavady and so it means that all of us, regardless of our disabilities, are able to partake in this sport.

In September 2006 I went to Bellarena full of confidence and looking forward to this new experience. I was met by my instructor for the day, Jay. We went into the clubroom and he gave me a cup of coffee. While sitting chatting, I said to Jay that I had been thinking on my way up that DSNI caters for all sorts of disabilities by providing all kinds of activities but how can they, as instructors, be prepared to cope with a situation like gliding, and with folk suffering from panic attacks. He looked at me, and said 'I do what I am doing now. I give you a cup of coffee, and chat and I have to decide how capable you are at obeying instructions'. I asked Jay if he did this full time, and whether they had special training to handle the disabled. He said he did not for they were all volunteers and that is why the airfield is only open at the weekends. I asked him what his job was and he said he worked for the Ministry of Defence. This just left me speechless, to think that these men have enough confidence and ability to accept us all as we were. After all they have no idea who is going to arrive at their door.

However off we went in a regular glider. Jay was sitting behind me, as the glider was dual control. We were hitched to a motorised plane and off we went, and once we were up 2,500 feet, we let the motorised leader plane go. We were now on our own. Oh, the view; the peace; the silence. It was magic. When approaching Mount Binevenagh the wind needs to rise in order to take us over the top. So of course up we went and looped the loop. And then round again. When gliding you never know how long the wind will allow you to stay up. It may be 20 minutes, or 40, or 60. You never know.

I remember the time many, many years ago, having to write at school about what kind of animal I wanted to be. I decided I wanted to be a bird – a seagull, because they have very few enemies. No one eats seagulls for they do not taste nice. So here I was – a seagull – floating on the wind. I did not need to flap my wings. I could just soar like them. Seagulls never falter; seagulls never stall, and neither did we. Seagulls never fly at night, and neither did we. Yes, I was an elegant, graceful seagull, even if it was just for a day.

Postscript
The tandem bike ride

As a child my brother and I had a tandem – a bike for two.

My brother Timothy and I used to ride it, Timothy in the front.

I often took a free ride, with my feet off the pedals – leaving Timothy to do all the work!

I did not realise then that Jesus was watching me – observing me.

Maybe I've learned a bit since then.

At first I saw God as my observer, my judge,

keeping track of all the things I did wrong,

so as to know whether I merited Heaven or hell when I died.

He was out there sort of like a President.

I recognised His picture when I saw it.

I did not really know Him.

But later on, when I met Jesus,

it seemed as if life was rather like a bike ride – a tandem bike,

and I noticed Jesus was on the back helping me pedal.

I don't know when he suggested that we changed places.

(Was it on 9th February when our Pastor spoke about Jesus

meeting His disciples and telling them to follow Him?

Pastor, I was listening – I do remember.

Or was it on the 20th of April when I met Sam Peacock?)

Jesus just smiles and says 'Keep pedalling'

and suggested that we changed places.

When I had control, I thought I knew the way.

It was rather boring and predictable.

I could see the shortest distance between two points, and go

there.

When Jesus took the lead, He knew the most delightful long

cuts,

up the mountains, and through the rocky places at breakneck

speeds.

Whoops, it was all I could do to hang on!

Although it looked like madness, He said 'Pedal'.

I worried and asked 'But where are you taking me?

He laughed and did not answer.

And I started to trust the Lord.

I forgot my boring life, and entered into the adventure
and when I said 'I was scared', He would lean back and pat my
hand.
He took me to meet people, like my Holywood Baptist friends,
who had the gifts I needed.
Gifts of healing; gifts of joy; gifts of love.
Most of all they accepted me as I was.

They gave me gifts to take on my life's journey.
Whoops, and we were off again!
Jesus said 'Give those gifts away. They are extra baggage,
too much to carry – so I gave them to people we met.
I found that in giving, I received,
and my burdens became lighter.

I did not trust Jesus to control my life for I thought He would
wreck it!
My life has not been the same since, but my Lord knows my
biking secrets.
He knows how to take the sharp corners; He knows how to jump
to clear the rocks below;
He knows how to fly the scary passages.
And now I have to learn to keep quiet, and listen.
I learn to pedal in the strangest of places – I am beginning to
enjoy the view.

I enjoy the cold breeze in my face with my new companion, Jesus Christ.

When I am sure I can do no more, He just smiles and says 'Keep pedalling'.

And that surely is what I have to learn to do.

Just keep on pedalling.